BLUES

COLLECTION
FOR GUITAR

by Ralph Agresta

Full-band backup to 45 extended jams in authentic blues styles.
Includes tips on scales and techniques to use with each track.
In standard notation and tablature.

T0078680

Amsco Publications
A Part of **The Music Sales Group**
New York/London/Paris/Sydney/Copenhagen/Berlin/Tokyo/Madrid

Cover photos from istockphoto.com

This book Copyright © 2010 by Amsco Publications,
A Division of Music Sales Corporation, New York, NY.

Order No. AM 1000472
International Standard Book Number: 978-0-8256-3741-4
HL Item Number: 14037686

Exclusive Distributor for the United States, Canada, Mexico and U.S. possessions:
Hal Leonard Corporation
7777 West Bluemound Road, Milwaukee, WI 53213 USA

Exclusive Distributors for the rest of the World:
Music Sales Limited
14-15 Berners Street, London W1T 3LJ England
Music Sales Pty. Limited
20 Resolution Drive, Caringbah, NSW 2229, Australia

Printed in the United States of America by
Vicks Lithograph and Printing Corporation

Contents

CD Track Listing

CD 1

1. Tuning
2. Twelve-Bar Blues in E
3. Twelve-Bar Blues in A
4. Twenty-four-Bar Blues in G
5. Twelve-Bar Rock 'n' Roll Blues in C
6. Twelve-Bar Jazzy Swing Feel Blues in B♭
7. Twelve-Bar Very Slow Swing in G
8. Twelve-Bar Boogie Shuffle in E
9. Twelve-Bar Funk Feel in C
10. Twelve-Bar Fast Boogie Shuffle with Modulations
11. Twelve-Bar Shuffle with Recurring Theme in D
12. Lucky Seven
13. Please Excuse Me
14. Livin' Roof
15. I Can't Take It Anymore
16. I Like the Weather
17. Mixed Feelings
18. R.A.'s Boogie in E
19. Stashbox
20. Slow Blues in F
21. Shortnin' Bread Blues
22. Rock You
23. My Muddy Waters

Musicians:
Ralph Agresta, guitar
Chris Carroll, drums
John Abbey, bass
Phil Ricciardi, keyboards

CD 2

1. Tuning
2. You Really Got to Love Me
3. I'll See Ya Later
4. Two-Room City Flat
5. Back Against the Wall
6. My Little Honey
7. Waiting on My Lady
8. Just One Nighht
9. No Credit
10. Plantation Blues
11. Candy Apple Coupe
12. I Can't Feel Your Love
13. Soon My Time Is Coming
14. Another Joy
15. Smokin' Solo
16. Talk to Your Baby
17. Slowhand Blues
18. Unchained Blues
19. Rotten to the Core
20. Too Much Blues
21. Still Got More Blues
22. The Bonnie/Smith Shuffle
23. No Apple Pies
24. Mrs. Sippy

Musicians:
Ralph Agresta, guitar & harmonica; keyboards (tracks 14–24)
Ernie Finamore, drums (tracks 2–13)
Phil Cimino, drums (tracks 14–24)
John Abbey, bass
Phil Ricciardi, keyboards (tracks 2–13)
Michael Alexander, saxophone

Introduction

Everyone knows that the best way to learn or improve improvising skills is to play with a live band, and now you can take advantage of this opportunity in the privacy of your own room. *Jam Trax* can be enjoyed by musicians of every level—more experienced players can use the CDs to experiment with new ideas and techniques or for warming up before gigs, and beginners can practice playing with a "live" band without the pressure that often comes from playing in front of other people.

Inside this book, you'll find a chord chart for each of the songs on the CDs. These charts show you what chords to play and how long to play them. Each song includes several suggested scale patterns, licks, and riffs that fit the progressions. Memorize these patterns and try to create your own solos by playing different note combinations. Experiment to discover which notes sound best over which chords. Be patient; most of the notes in any given key will go quite nicely with the corresponding featured chord progression.

Let's discuss some notation basics that will help the beginning player follow the chord charts. First, music is divided into *measures* (blocks of time). These measures—or *bars*, as they are often called—are also divided into smaller lengths of time called *beats*. Most of the tunes have four beats to each measure (notice the four slashes in each measure). The simplest approach is to strum one chord for each beat:

The symbol 𝄆 marks the point to which you must return after reaching the symbol 𝄇. These are called *repeat signs*. Playing through the section of music between the repeat signs once is called playing a *chorus*. Each song is marked to indicate how many choruses are to be played. Repeated sections frequently have different endings, which are numbered accordingly:

A *coda* is usually a few bars of music that ends a song. The abbreviation *D.S. al Coda* ("from the sign to the coda") means to jump back to the symbol 𝄋 (the "sign"), play through until you see the coda symbol ⊕, and then skip to the section marked ⊕ **Coda** to end the tune:

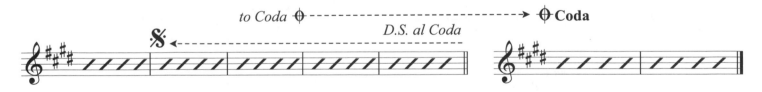

The 45 rhythm tracks on the two CDs provided will allow musicians at every level to practice soloing ideas and techniques while playing with a live back-up band. All of these progressions have served as the basis for some of the greatest songs in the history of popular music. CD 1 contains mostly traditional 12- and 24-bar blues progressions, while CD 2 focuses on the Chicago style and more modern blues sounds. As you jam along with *Jam Trax*, keep in mind that it is not uncommon for more than one instrument to be playing lead parts and solos at the same time. So, in addition to playing in the more obvious spaces, do not shy away from adding tasteful licks in the more musically busy areas.

E Blues Scale Patterns

Pattern 1

Pattern 2

Pattern 3

Pattern 4

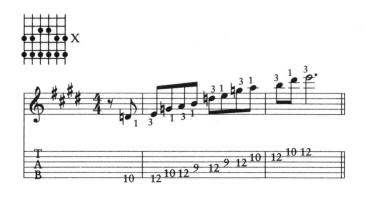

Twelve-Bar Blues in E

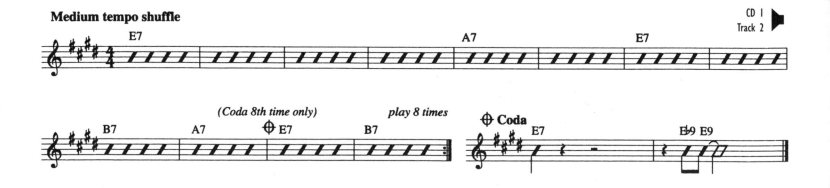

A Blues Scale Patterns

Pattern 1

Pattern 2

Pattern 3

Pattern 4

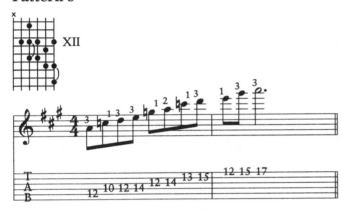

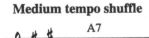

Twelve-Bar Blues in A

CD 1
Track 3

(Coda 8th time only)

Medium tempo shuffle

play 8 times   **Coda**

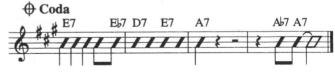

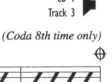

G Blues Scale Patterns

Pattern 1

Pattern 2

Pattern 3

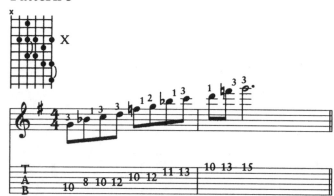

Pattern 4

Twenty-four–Bar Blues in G

This twenty-four-bar blues in G has a rock 'n' roll feel similar to an old Rolling Stones tune, "Off the Hook," or to the Stones' version of Bobby Womack's "It's All Over Now." The fifth chorus may remind you of the Beatles' "She's a Woman." Notice the eight-bar intro and the extended coda.

CD 1
Track 4

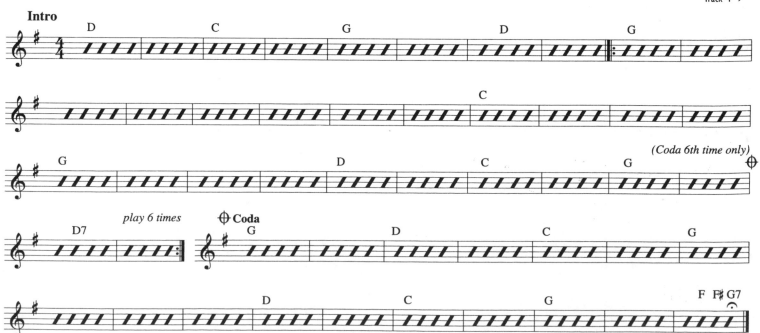

C Blues Scale Patterns

Pattern 1

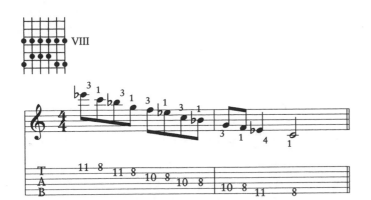

Pattern 2

Pattern 3

Pattern 4

Twelve-Bar Rock 'n' Roll Blues in C

Here's a twelve-bar progression that has a different straight-time rock feel. Think of Little Richard's "Lucille" or the Beatles' version of Larry Williams's "Dizzy Miss Lizzy." This example might even remind you of the Beatles' "You Can't Do That."

CD 1
Track 5

B♭ Blues Scale Patterns

Pattern 1

Pattern 2

Pattern 3

Pattern 4

Twelve-Bar Jazzy Swing Feel in B♭

Here's yet another twelve-bar blues with a completely different feel. This time you'll hear a medium tempo swing. Notice the slightly more complex chord progression. Don't worry! The blues scales provided here will also work well over these jazz-influenced chord changes.

CD 1
Track 6

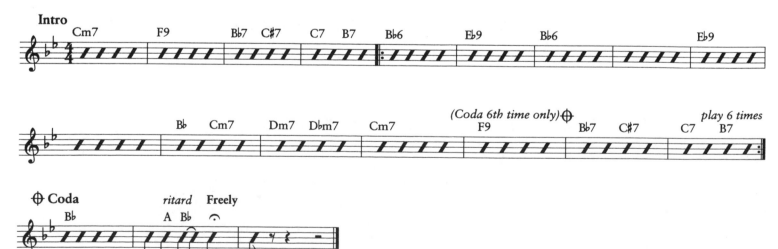

Twelve-Bar Very Slow Swing in G

This example is a slow blues in G that will remind you of the
Allman Brothers' version of the classic "Stormy Monday."

CD 1
Track 7

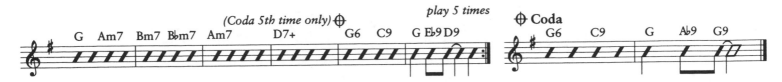

Twelve-Bar Boogie Shuffle in E

There are many ways to interpret the blues. Here's one that
hints at David Bowie's "Gene Genie." This may also remind
you of Booker T.'s "Green Onions," played frequently by Paul
Shaffer and the CBS Orchestra.

CD 1
Track 8

Twelve-Bar Funk Feel in C

A more rhythmic approach to your playing will work well over
this twelve-bar funk groove.

CD 1
Track 9

F Blues Scale Patterns

Pattern 1

Pattern 2

Pattern 3

Pattern 4

Twelve-Bar Fast Boogie Shuffle With Modulations

For this example we've combined three 12-bar choruses, each played twice and each in a different key! (*Modulation* is the process of changing from one key to another.) The second ending riff is in standard notation and guitar tablature.

CD 1
Track 10

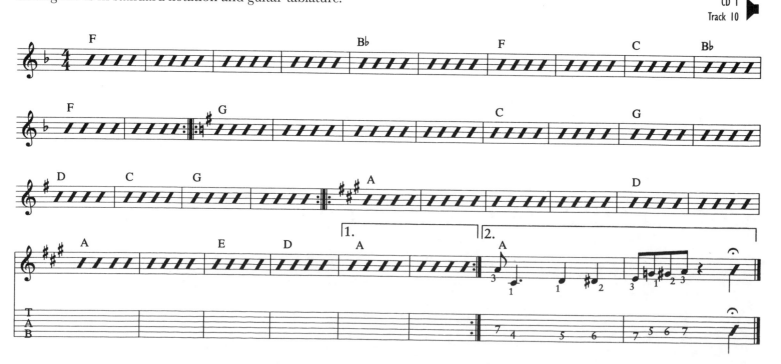

D Blues Scale Patterns

Pattern 1

Pattern 2

Pattern 3

Pattern 4

Twelve-Bar Shuffle Feel With Recurring Theme in D

Lastly, another twelve-bar shuffle. This one's in D and has a recurring theme, or "main riff." You can solo over and around this riff. Also, you can play rhythm behind it and solo over the choruses whenever I play the chords. You can even try to play the theme in unison or up an octave.

CD 1
Track 11

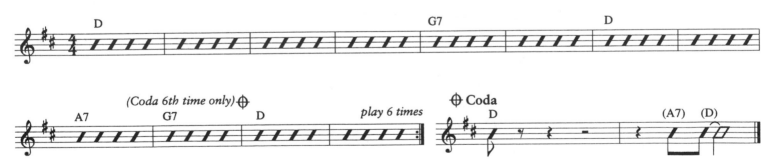

Theme or "Main Riff"

14

Lucky Seven

Pattern 1:

G minor pentatonic "box" pattern (1st position)

Pattern 2:

G minor pentatonic "box" pattern (IIIrd position)

As you know, "position" in guitar playing refers to the fret that the index finger lies across.

Pattern 3:

G minor pentatonic scale with extension

Pattern 4:

G minor pentatonic scale with extension (VIIIth position)

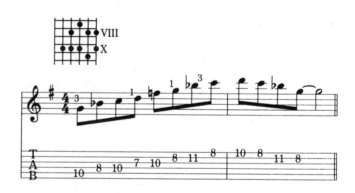

Pattern 5:

G minor pentatonic scale with extension and unison bends

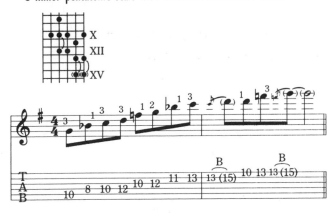

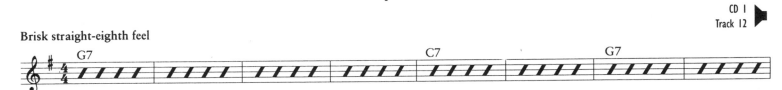

Lucky Seven

CD 1
Track 12

Brisk straight-eighth feel

Please Excuse Me

Pattern 1:

E blues scale with pickup note

The only difference between this particular version of the blues scale and a minor pentatonic scale is the addition of the flatted fifth (here a B♭).

Pattern 2:

E minor pentatonic scale with extension and quarter-tone bend

A quarter-tone bend means that you just tweak the pitch a little, not enough to reach the next note up.

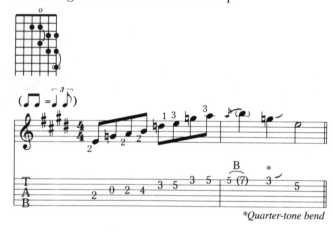

Quarter-tone bend

Pattern 3:

E blues riff with combined minor and major thirds

Pattern 4:
E minor pentatonic scale with bend

Pattern 5:
E minor pentatonic scale with extension and bend

Please Excuse Me

CD 1
Track 13

Moderate shuffle

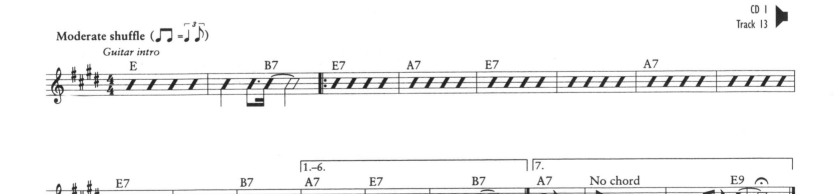

Livin' Roof

Pattern 1:

A minor pentatonic box pattern (Vth position)

Pattern 2:

A blues scale with combined major and minor thirds

Pattern 3:

Three-octave A minor pentatonic scale with combined major and minor thirds

Pattern 4:
A minor pentatonic scale

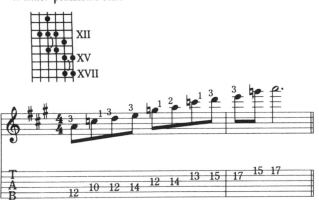

Pattern 5:
A major pentatonic scale with slides and hammeron

Pattern 6:
Three-octave A major pentatonic scale

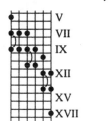

Livin' Roof

CD 1
Track 14

Moderate straight funk

I Can't Take It Anymore

Pattern 1:

G blues scale with combined minor and major thirds

Pattern 2:

Mixed major/minor mode blues pattern in G with bends

Pattern 3:

Three-octave G major pentatonic scale

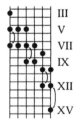

Pattern 4:
Two-octave G major pentatonic scale with extension

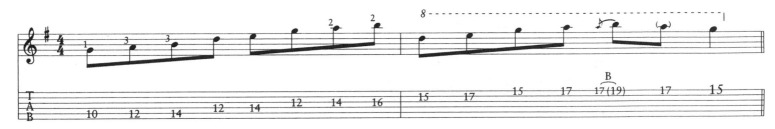

Pattern 5:
G major pentatonic box pattern

I Can't Take It Anymore

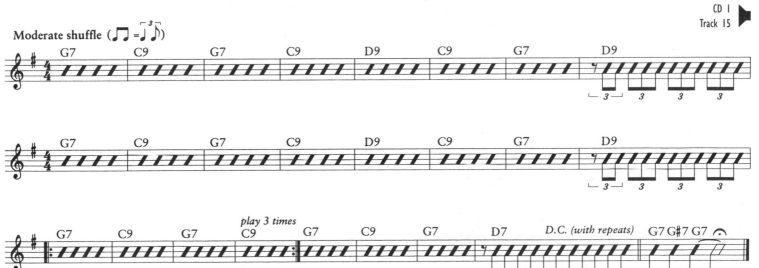

I Like the Weather

Pattern 1:

C minor pentatonic scale

Pattern 2:

C minor pentatonic scale with single-note extension

Pattern 3:

C major pentatonic box pattern

Pattern 4:
C minor pentatonic scale with mixed major and minor thirds and extension

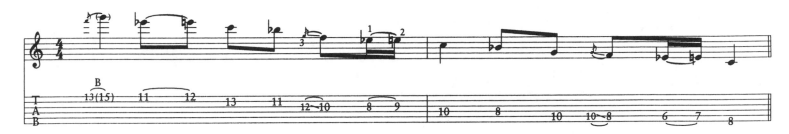

I Like the Weather

CD 1
Track 16

Moderate straight-eighth feel

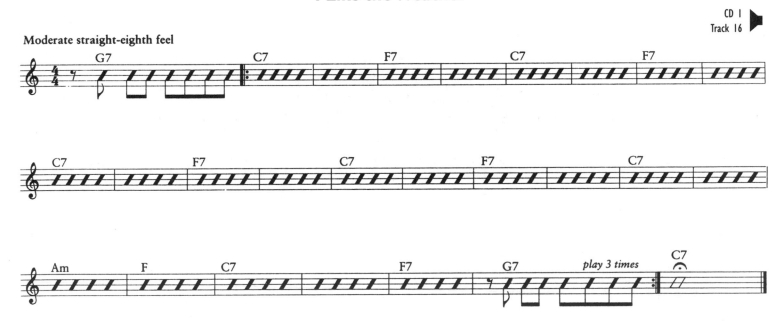

Mixed Feelings

Pattern 1:

D minor pentatonic scale

Pattern 2:

D minor pentatonic scale with extension and unison bend

Pattern 3:

D minor pentatonic scale with extension

Pattern 4:
D blues scale with pickup note

Mixed Feelings

R.A.'s Boogie in E

Pattern 1:

E minor pentatonic riff

Pattern 2:

E blues riff with repeated note

Pattern 3:

E major pentatonic scale with unison bend

Pattern 4:

Minor pentatonic riff with double stops and quarter-tone bends

Pattern 5:

Chromatic hammeron riff in E

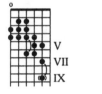

R.A.'s Boogie in E

CD 1
Track 18

Fast shuffle

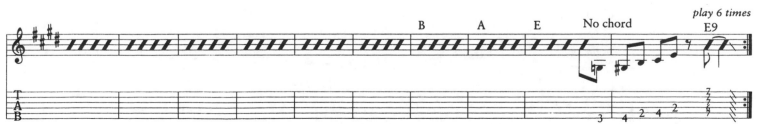

Stashbox

Pattern 1:

A major pentatonic scale

Pattern 2:

A major riff

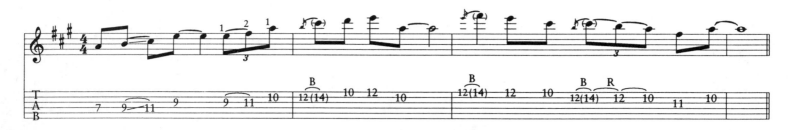

Pattern 3:

Mixed major/minor mode pattern in A (Vth position), B (VIIth pos.), and
E (XIIth pos.)

Play this over measures 31 through 34. All the riffs come out of
the same fretboard pattern. Just slide your index finger to the
right positions.

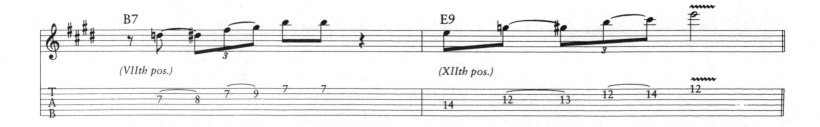

Stashbox

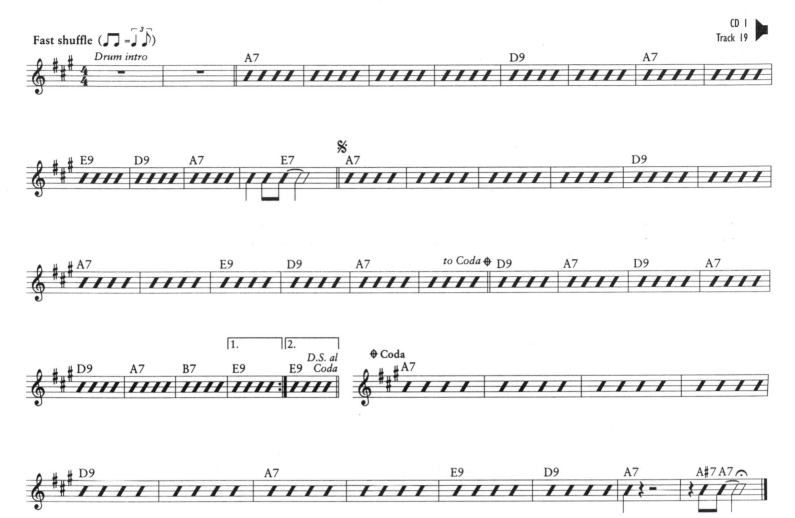

Slow Blues in F

Pattern 1:

Mixed major/minor mode pattern in F with extension

Pattern 2:

F minor pentatonic riff with mixed major and minor thirds

Pattern 3:

Mixed major/minor mode blues riff

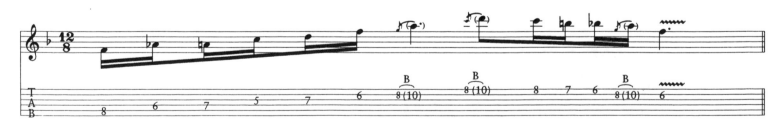

Pattern 4:

Two-octave F major pentatonic scale

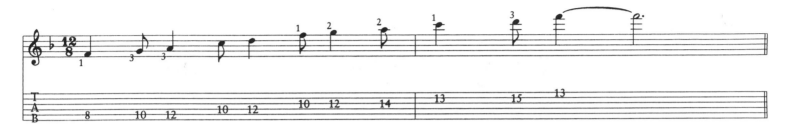

Pattern 5:

Two-octave F minor pentatonic scale with pickup note

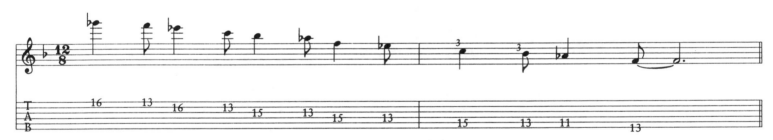

Slow Blues in F

CD I
Track 20

Shortnin' Bread Blues

Pattern 1:

Two B♭ major pentatonic riffs

Note the mixed major and minor thirds in measure two.

Pattern 2:

Mixed major/minor mode blues riff in B♭

Pattern 3:

Riff in B♭ with mixed major and minor thirds

Pattern 4:
B♭ major pentatonic scale with combined major/minor mode extension

Shortnin' Bread Blues

CD 1
Track 21

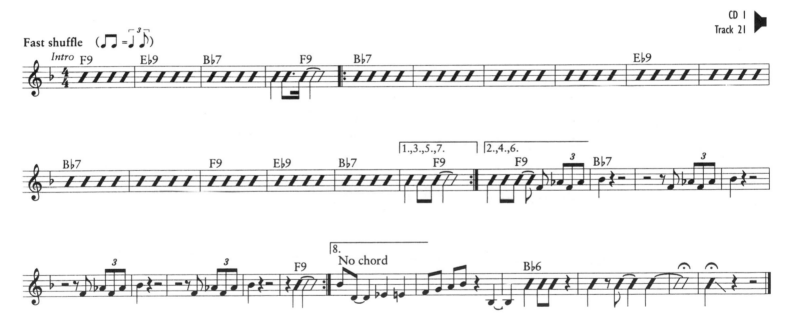

Rock You

Pattern 1:

Two-octave D minor pentatonic scale with bend

Pattern 2:

Two-octave D minor pentatonic scale with extension

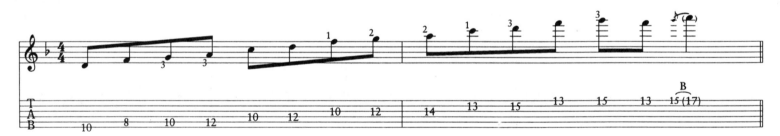

Pattern 3:

D minor pentatonic box pattern (Xth position)

Pattern 4:

Descending three-octave D blues scale

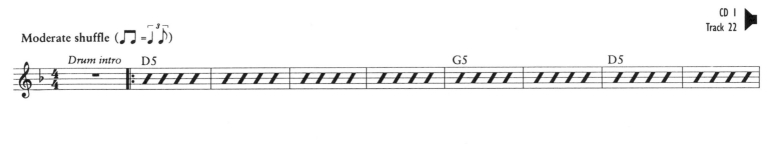

Rock You

CD 1
Track 22

Moderate shuffle

36

My Muddy Waters

Pattern 1:

E blues scale with bends

Pattern 2:

E minor pentatonic scale

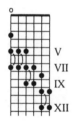

Pattern 3:

Blues riff in E

Pattern 4:

Mixed major/minor mode blues riff in E with double and triple stops

Pattern 5:

Double-stop blues riff

Try this one over the last two bars of the tune (i.e., the third ending).

My Muddy Waters

CD 1
Track 23

You Really Got to Love Me

Pattern 1:

Two-octave A minor pentatonic scale

We'll begin with the obligatory A minor pentatonic scale. This two-octave version contains a fingerboard slide that will allow you to play the low C on the third fret, a common blues fingering.

Pattern 2:

A minor pentatonic riff sample

Try playing this over the first four bars of A7, then play through the rest of the progression by creating simple variations on the main riff (measure 1). Chicago blues guitarists tend to play in the upper registers of these scales. Don't be afraid to play very simply on the top three or four strings.

Pattern 3:

A blues scale pattern with mixed major and minor thirds

The term "blues scale" is used rather loosely, but in general it designates a pentatonic scale with extra chromatic notes added in. These are often flatted fifths, but the mixing of major and minor thirds is also critical in achieving that "bluesy" sound. This pattern goes down into the bass register, but there is normally no need to go below the middle A (4th string, 7th fret), so stay in the higher octave.

Pattern 4:

Riff sample

Here is a simple blues phrase that with or without variation can
be used to create an entire twelve-bar solo.

You Really Got to Love Me

CD 2
Track 2

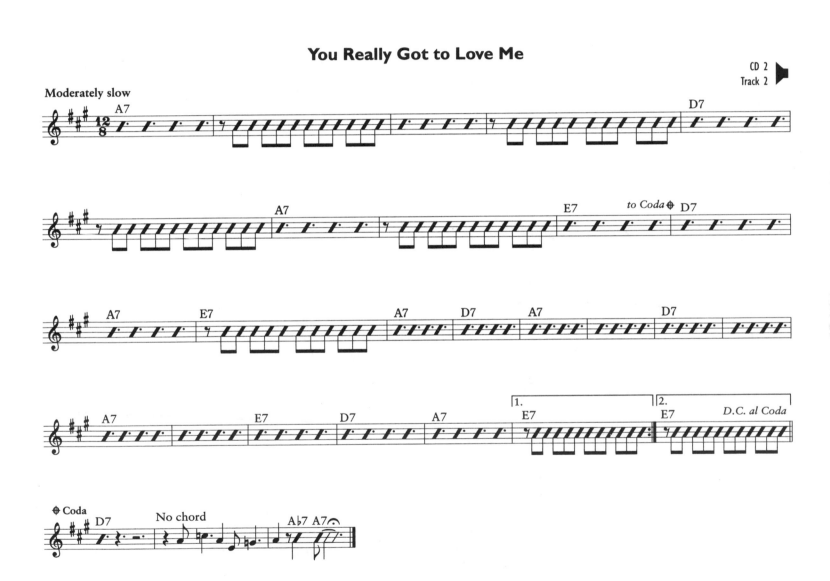

I'll See Ya Later

Pattern 1:

Two-octave G minor pentatonic scale

Here we see the box pattern in IIIrd position (key of G), minus the pickup note.

Pattern 2:

G minor pentatonic scale with mixed major and minor thirds and extension

Pattern 3:

Single-octave G blues scale

Pattern 4:

Riff sample

This riff sample combines notes taken from the previous three patterns.

I'll See Ya Later

This track provides a good example of an arrangement in which the lead guitarist must employ discretion, respecting the sax and harmonica while looking for spaces in the music in which to inject his own solos and licks.

CD 2
Track 3

Two-Room City Flat

Pattern 1:

Another fingering for the G minor pentatonic scale

Pattern 2:

Riff sample

This is a busy slide lick using notes taken from the above pattern. Keep the timing loose and free. You can actually cram as many or as few of the four-note phrases (you'll find six of them in measure 1), into any number of bars with any rhythmic treatment you like.

Patterns 3 and 4:

Two-octave G blues scale in both IIIrd and XVth positions

pattern 3

(IIIrd position)

pattern 4

(XVth position)

Pattern 5:

Riff sample

This simple blues lick features a repeated upper-octave G note.

Two-Room City Flat

Here again, respect the piano as you add your lead guitar part. Your leads should complement the track's mood. Also notice the unexpected yet stylistically appropriate key change in the coda. The suggested guitar lick (in G major) will fit nicely in the open space left for it in the track. Of course, you should also try your own licks here.

CD 2
Track 4

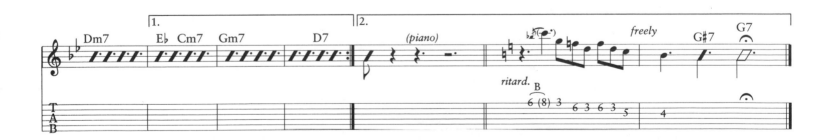

Back Against the Wall

Pattern 1:

Two-octave E minor pentatonic scale

Pattern 2:

E minor pentatonic scale with extension

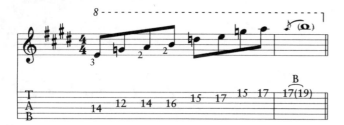

Pattern 3:

Two-octave E minor pentatonic scale with extension and unison bends

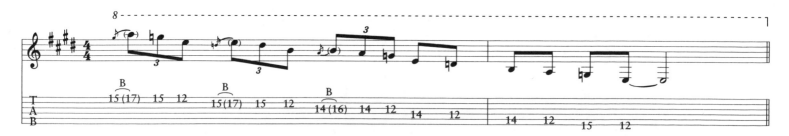

Pattern 4:

Riff sample

This twelve-bar solo shows how to establish, develop, and resolve a simple musical motif.

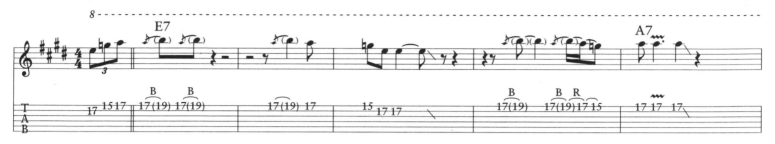

Back Against the Wall

CD 2
Track 5

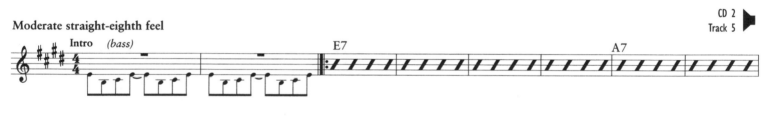

My Little Honey

Pattern 1:

D blues scale

Pattern 2:

Mixed major- and minor-mode blues pattern

Pattern 3:

D minor pentatonic scale with mixed major and minor thirds

Played with bends and slides, this pattern will work well in this track's major blues setting.

Pattern 4:

Riff sample

These few bars use ideas taken from the first three patterns.

My Little Honey

In the second section of this track you'll hear a clean second lead guitar part. Choose a guitar sound that will complement it and jam along. Use taste but don't be afraid to play right beside the second lead part.

CD 2
Track 6

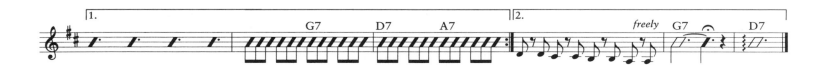

48

Waiting on My Lady

Pattern 1:

Two-octave C blues scale with pickup note

Pattern 2:

Two-octave F blues scale with pickup note

Pattern 3:

Two-octave G blues scale with pickup note

Patterns 4, 5, and 6:

Riff samples

Check out these three double-stop riff ideas (one for each chord in the progression).

pattern 4

pattern 5

pattern 6

Waiting on My Lady

CD 2
Track 7

Just One Night

Pattern 1:

G major pentatonic scale with extension

Pattern 2:

Two-octave G major pentatonic scale

Pattern 3:

Riff sample

Try these eight bars over the intro chords. You can also try to apply the ideas found in this sample to the rest of the tune.

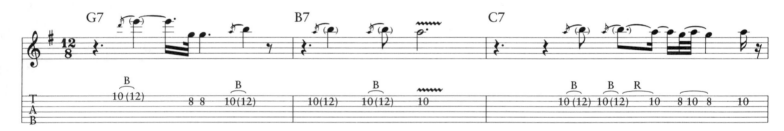

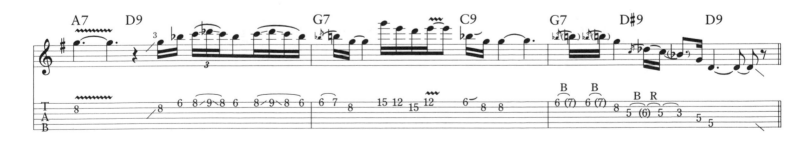

Just One Night

No Credit

Pattern 1:

F minor pentatonic scale with pickup note

This example shows the scale as used over the F7, B♭7, and
C7 chords.

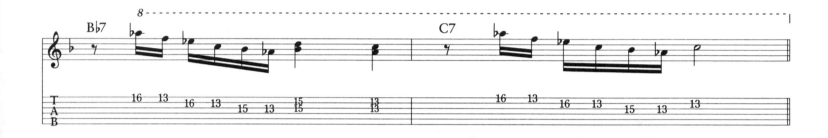

Pattern 2:

F minor pentatonic pattern

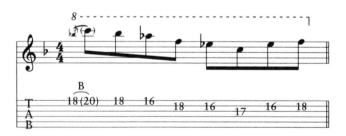

Pattern 3:

Twelve-bar riff sample

This sample is based on the notes found in the above pattern.

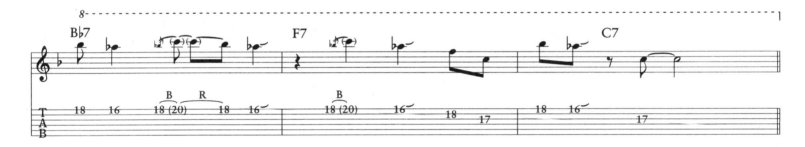

No Credit

CD 2
Track 9

Medium straight-eighth feel

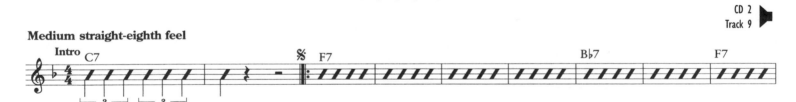

to Coda ⊕
(last time only)

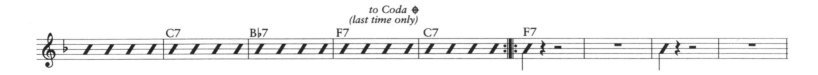

1.

2. *D.S. al Coda*

⊕ **Coda**

Plantation Blues

Pattern 1:

C7 double-stop riff

Pattern 2:

Another C7 double-stop riff

Pattern 3:

Chuck Berry-style double-stop riff

Pattern 4:

Hammered double-stop riff sample

Plantation Blues

You can also use scales and licks from "Waiting on My Lady"
on this track, since both tunes are in C.

CD 2
Track 10

Candy Apple Coupe

Pattern 1:

Riff sample

Shown here over the I(E7), IV(A7), and V(B7) chords in the key of E is the main riff that the guitar and bass play throughout the track.

Pattern 2:

Riff sample

This riff sample uses major- and minor-mode notes. It's really more of a rockabilly riff as such, but the pattern can be used in a more traditional bluesy way.

Pattern 3:

Two-octave E major pentatonic scale with extension

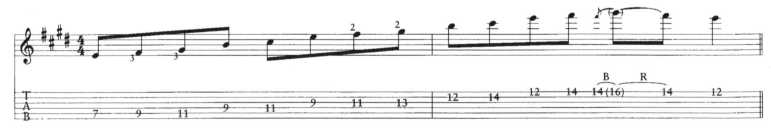

Candy Apple Coupe

CD 2
Track 11

I Can't Feel Your Love

Pattern 1:

Two-octave A blues scale

Pattern 2:

Riff sample

This A blues riff features slides and pulloffs.

Pattern 3:

Two-octave A minor pentatonic scale with extension

Pattern 4:

Riff sample

This next sample is basically two riffs, both featuring bends,
releases, and pulloffs.

I Can't Feel Your Love

The minor-mode scales and samples that we looked at for "You
Really Got to Love Me" can be used for this jam in the key of
A minor.

CD 2
Track 12

Soon My Time Is Coming

Pattern 1:

Two-octave B♭ minor pentatonic scale with pickup note

Pattern 2:

Riff sample

This stylistically correct riff sample is just one of the endless
ways in which you can use the B♭ minor pentatonic scale above.

Pattern 3:

B♭ minor pentatonic scale with extension

Pattern 4:

Riff sample

This lick shows one way of using the notes in the above pattern.

Soon My Time Is Coming

CD 2
Track 13

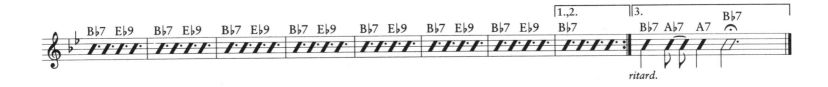

Another Joy

Pattern 1:

E minor pentatonic scale (two-octave)

Below are two versions of the common *pentatonic* (five-note) *scale* covering two octaves. This is often called a *box pattern*. In the key of E, it may be played in the first and twelfth positions.

Pattern 2:

E blues scale

Adding the flatted fifth to the standard pentatonic scale produces what is traditionally called the *blues scale*. In the key of E, the flatted fifth is Bb. As with the minor pentatonic scale, this blues-scale pattern may be played in the first and twelfth positions.

Pattern 3:

E minor pentatonic scale with extension

Here is a different pattern for the E minor pentatonic scale which covers one and one-half octaves.

Pattern 4:

E minor pentatonic scale (three-octave)

Pattern 4 is a pentatonic pattern which covers three octaves, from the open sixth string to the first string, twelfth fret.

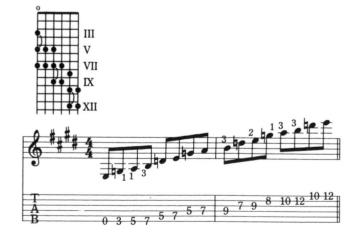

Patterns 5 and 6:

E major pentatonic riffs

The following licks are from two similar major-pentatonic patterns. Both work well when soloing over "Another Joy."

pattern 5

pattern 6

Pattern 7:

Mixed major- and minor-mode riff

Here is a riff that combines Patterns 1 and 3. This riff also includes the major third (G♯) to produce an example of how a modern blues player such as Stevie Ray Vaughn would use these scales.

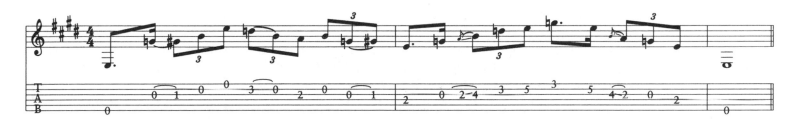

This jam is based on the common twelve-bar I-IV-V chord progression, which is the main progression used in both modern and classic blues music.

Another Joy

CD 2
Track 14

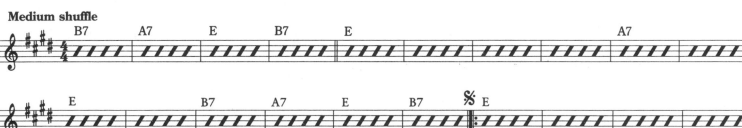

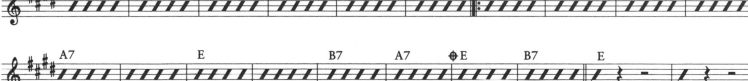

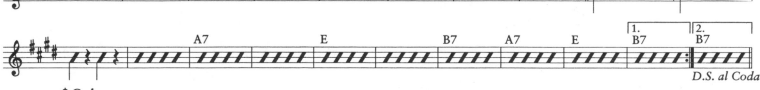

D.S. al Coda

Smokin' Solo

Robert Cray's "Smoking Gun" inspired this next jam. Since we're playing in the key of E minor, Patterns 1 through 4 from "Another Joy" may be applied here.

Pattern 1:

E minor pentatonic scale (two-octave)

Add this version of the two-octave pentatonic scale to your collection.

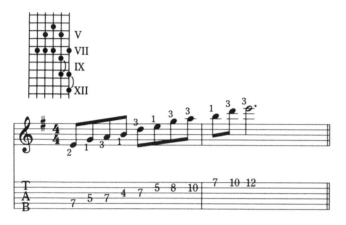

Pattern 2:

A natural minor scale (two-octave)

This two-octave A natural minor scale is in fifth position and may be used to play over the Am7 chord in measures 13 through 16. You can also move this scale pattern up to twelfth position to play over the Em7 chord in measures 17 through 20.

A simple way to play over the chord changes in measures 21 through 24 is to *transpose* (change key of) Pattern 1 from "Another Joy" by sliding it to ninth position when playing over the C#m7. Then slide this pattern down to second position to play over the F#m7.

Likewise, a transposed Pattern 6 may be used to play over the F# and B9 chords: Slide Pattern 6 up one whole-step (two frets) to transpose it from the key of E to the key of F# where the pattern will begin in ninth position. To play over the B9 chord, slide Pattern 6 down five half-steps (five frets) from the key of E to the key of B, where the pattern will begin in second position.

C# Minor Pentatonic

F# Minor Pentatonic

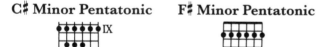

F# Major Pentatonic

B Major Pentatonic

Smokin' Solo

CD 2
Track 15

Medium straight-eighth feel

Em7 ... Em7

Am7 ... Em7

C#m7 F# F#m7 B9 Em7 *play three times* *play four times* Em9

Talk to Your Baby

Patterns 1 and 2:

A minor pentatonic and blues scales

pattern 1

pattern 2

Pattern 3:

Mixing A major and A minor modes

By adding major-mode elements (major thirds, major sixths, and ninths) to the blues scale, you can easily add a little more color to your solos. Notice that in this descending pattern I've reversed the order of the thirds. This is because it usually sounds better to use the minor third to lead up to the major third.

Pattern 4:

A minor pentatonic scale (two-octave)

Pattern 5:

A major pentatonic scale (two-octave)

Pattern 6:

A major pentatonic scale (three-octave)

All of the scales and patterns that have been suggested for use over the A chord may be used over the B chord simply by raising them one whole-step (two frets).

Patterns 7 and 8:

Major-mode riffs on E and D

These two riffs both contain minor-third-to-major-third hammerons. Use these licks over the V (E) and IV (D) chords.

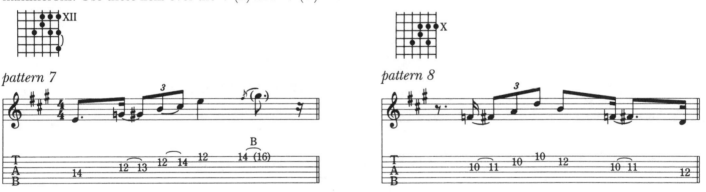

Talk to Your Baby

CD 2
Track 16

Slowhand Blues

Since "Slowhand Blues" is in A minor, all of the A minor and
A minor pentatonic patterns that we've looked at so far may be
used to build a solo (see "Smokin' Solo," Pattern 9 and "Talk to
Your Baby," Patterns 1 through 4). Any of the E minor patterns
from "Another Joy" (Patterns 1 through 4 and Pattern 7) may be
used over the E7♯9.

Patterns 1 and 2:

A natural minor scale with extension and A minor arpeggio

pattern 1

pattern 2

Pattern 3:

Riff combining patterns 1 and 2

Pattern 4:

G Mixolydian scale

Try this G Mixolydian scale when playing over the G7sus4 and
Em7 chords.

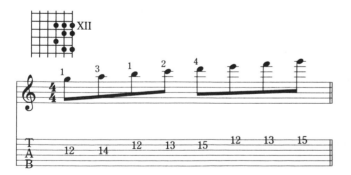

Pattern 5:

F major seven arpeggio with major-scale extension

Patterns 5 and 6 may be used to play over the F chords in "Slowhand Blues." Be careful not to create unwanted dissonance by dwelling on the E note in Pattern 5 when using this pattern over the F chord.

Pattern 6:

F major pentatonic scale with extension

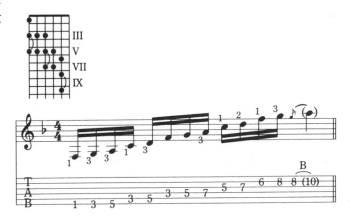

Slowhand Blues

CD 2
Track 17

Slow straight-eighth feel

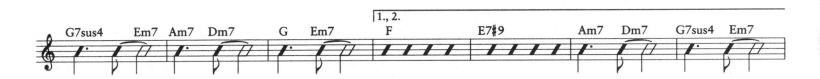

Unchained Blues

Patterns 1 and 2:

C natural minor scale and C natural minor scale with pickup and extension

pattern 1

pattern 2

Patterns 3 and 4:

C minor arpeggio riff and C natural minor scale

Pattern 3 is a simple C Minor arpeggio that leads nicely into a descending riff ending on the flatted seventh (B♭).

Pattern 4 is another way to play a one-octave C minor scale, this one starts in third position.

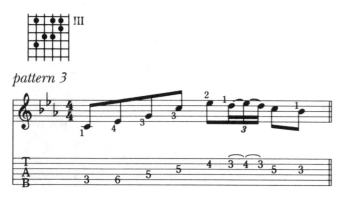

pattern 3

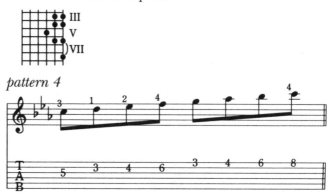

pattern 4

Pattern 5:

C minor pentatonic "box-pattern" riff

You can think of the key of C minor as three half-steps (three frets) higher than the key of A minor. Any of the A minor patterns diagramed with "Talk to Your Baby" and "Slowhand Blues" may be transposed to C minor simply by sliding them up three frets. It will sound fine if you stay with C minor patterns straight through the G♯ and G7 chords, but you may want to play directly over these changes by lowering an A blues pattern one half-step (one fret) for the G♯ and one whole-step (two frets) for the G7s.

Unchained Blues

CD 2
Track 18

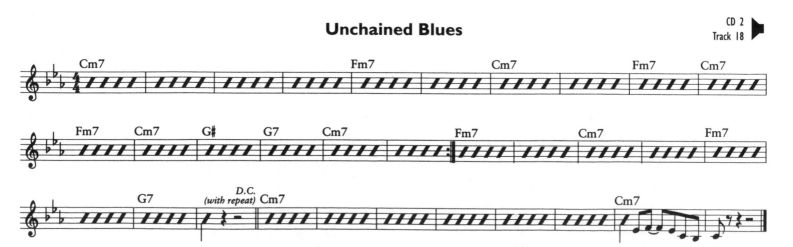

Rotten to the Core

Based on an old Delta blues *bottleneck* (or *slide)* guitar lick, this tip of the hat to George Thorogood's "Bad to the Bone" should be played with either a glass or metal slide in *Open-G* tuning.

Pattern 1:

Open-G tuning

To produce Open-G tuning, tune your first, fifth, and sixth strings each down one whole-step.

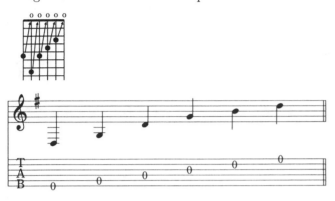

Pattern 2:

The "theme" riff

Pattern 3:

Theme-riff variation 1

Pattern 4:

Theme-riff variation 2

Pattern 5:

Theme-riff variation 3

Pattern 6:

Theme-riff variation 4

Pattern 7:
Theme-riff variation 5

Although "Rotten to the Core" is nothing more than a two-measure vamp on G repeated twenty times, the chart below reflects the changing textures of the recorded track.

Rotten to the Core

CD 2
Track 19

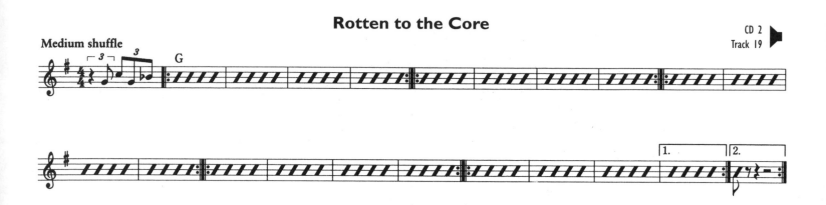

Too Much Blues

To play the blues in the key of D, you should again transpose all of your major and minor pentatonic and blues patterns.

To transpose an A pattern to D, move it up the neck five half-steps (five frets) or down the neck seven half-steps (seven frets).

Pattern 1:
D major scale with pickup and chromatic embellishments

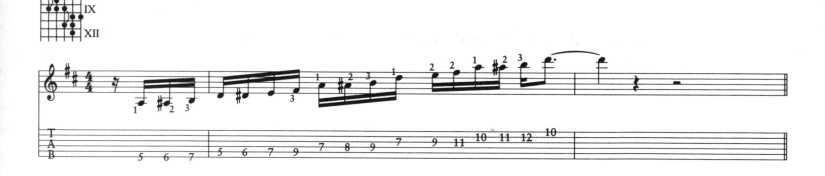

Pattern 2:
D major chromatic riff

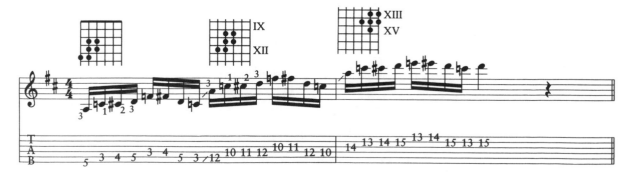

Pattern 3:

D major riff with bent double-stop

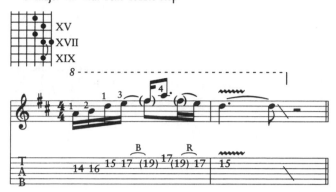

This track might remind you of one of Jeff Healey's more popular songs, "I Think I Love You Too Much." On the other hand, it might also remind you of a modern version of Cream's "Strange Brew," or even "Born under a Bad Sign" (which was covered by Cream and, more recently, by another truly fine modern blues player, Robben Ford).

Too Much Blues

CD 2
Track 20

Brisk straight-eighth feel

Still Got More Blues

Gary Moore released a very modern sounding production of a song called "Still Got the Blues" which features some blistering lead guitar solos. This variation has been stripped down to a basic guitar-bass-drums backing track that retains the same feel and similar chord changes.

For this one, you may use two of the previously encountered scale groups. First, transpose all of the A-minor patterns up one whole-step (two frets) to put them in B minor. Second, since B minor is the *relative minor* of D major, you may use any of the D-major patterns that you used in "Too Much Blues."

Pattern 1:

D major seven arpeggio with chromatic embellishments and descending D major scale

Pattern 2:

G major pentatonic scale and G major arpeggio

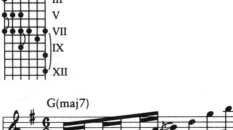

Pattern 3:

B minor pentatonic scale with flatted fifth and sharped fifth

Still Got More Blues

CD 2
Track 21

The Bonnie/Smith Shuffle

To play in the key of B♭, we'll transpose the A major and A minor pentatonic and A blues patterns up one half-step (one fret).

Pattern 1:

Double-stop riff with slides

Pattern 2:

B♭ major/minor riff

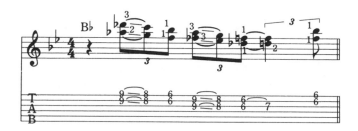

Pattern 3:

F major pentatonic scale with slides

Pattern 4:

Shuffle riff

The success of Bonnie Raitt's album *Nick of Time* has helped to keep the blues alive and well in today's often trendy musical scene. The thematic riff featured in this next jam is akin to the one heard in Raitt's "A Thing Called Love." Coincidentally, a similar lick may be heard in Aerosmith's "Same Old Song and Dance."

The Bonnie/Smith Shuffle

CD 2
Track 22

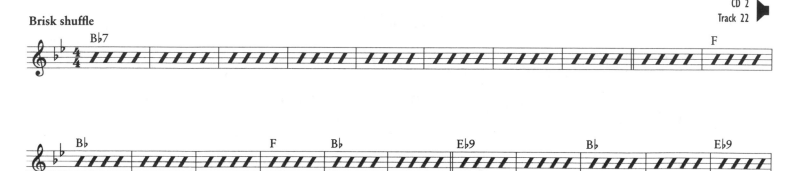

No Apple Pies

This example was included to represent the more modern approach to playing the blues over a more rock-like feel in the rhythm section. An example of this may be heard on Eric Clapton's "No Alibis" from his *Journeyman* album.

You may play over the bulk of this tune by using the same D-major patterns and scales that we used for "Too Much Blues." Notice, however, that as the last chord of sections B and C are A major chords (measures 16 and 25), you may want to hit a note or two from the A chord (A, C#, or E).

Pattern 1:

A chord shapes

Here are four A major chord shapes from which you can select chord tones to use in measures 16 and 25.

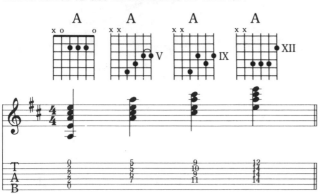

Pattern 2:

G major pentatonic scale

Here's a handy position for use in measure 17.

Pattern 3:

D major pentatonic riff

Pattern 4:

D major/minor riff

No Apple Pies

CD 2
Track 23

Medium straight-eighth feel

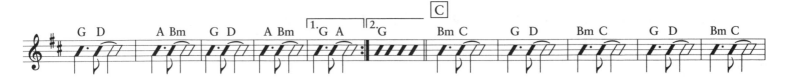

(rit. - - -)

Mrs. Sippy

"Mrs. Sippy" is a ZZ Top-style blues boogie in the keys of A
and C. Again, you can use all of your A major and A minor
pentatonic and A blues patterns and transpose them up three
half-steps (three frets) for the key of C.

Pattern 1:
A minor pentatonic riff

Pattern 2:
C minor pentatonic riff

Pattern 3:
C minor pentatonic riff with bent double-stop

Mrs. Sippy

CD 2
Track 24

Chords

V = fret number
x = don't play string

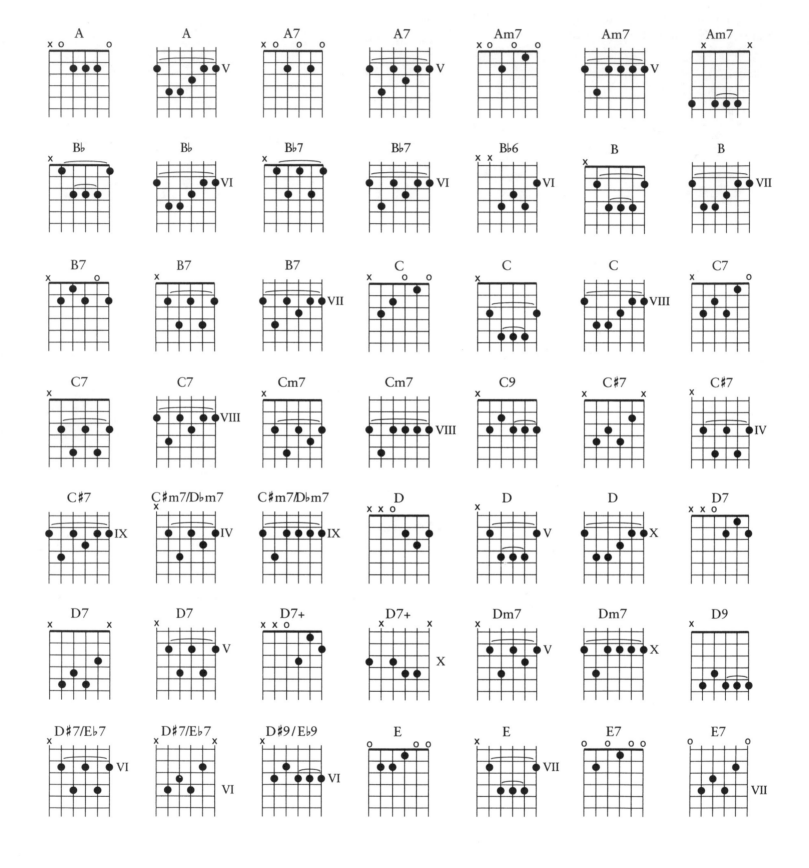

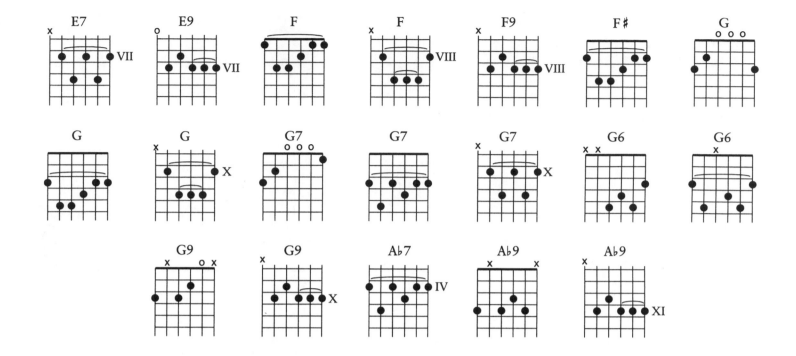